A Hippopotamusn't
AND OTHER ANIMAL POEMS

by J. Patrick Lewis ▾ *pictures by* Victoria Chess

A Puffin Pied Piper

PUFFIN PIED PIPER BOOKS
Published by the Penguin Group
Penguin Books USA Inc., 375 Hudson Street, New York, New York 10014, U.S.A.
Penguin Books Ltd, 27 Wrights Lane, London W8 5TZ, England
Penguin Books Australia Ltd, Ringwood, Victoria, Australia
Penguin Books Canada Ltd, 10 Alcorn Avenue, Toronto, Ontario, Canada M4V 3B2
Penguin Books (N.Z.) Ltd, 182–190 Wairau Road, Auckland 10, New Zealand
Penguin Books Ltd, Registered Offices: Harmondsworth, Middlesex, England

Originally published in hardcover by
Dial Books for Young Readers
A Division of Penguin Books USA Inc.

Library of Congress Catalog Card Number: 87-24579
Printed in Hong Kong by South China Printing Company (1988) Limited
First Puffin Pied Piper Printing 1994
ISBN 0-14-055273-1
10 9 8 7 6 5 4 3 2 1

A Pied Piper Book is a registered trademark of
Dial Books for Young Readers,
A Division of Penguin Books USA Inc.,
® TM 1,163,686 and ® TM 1,054,312.

A HIPPOPOTAMUSN'T
is also available in hardcover from
Dial Books for Young Readers.

For Beth, Matt, and Leigh Ann
J. P. L.

Pop, with love
V. C.

A TOMCAT IS

Night watchman of corners
Caretaker of naps
Leg-wrestler of pillows
Depresser of laps.

A master at whining
And dining on mouse
Afraid of the shadows
That hide in the house.

The bird-watching bandit
On needle-point claws
The chief of detectives
On marshmallow paws.

A crafty yarn-spinner
A stringer high-strung
A buttermilk mustache
A sandpaper tongue.

The dude in the alley
The duke on the couch
Affectionate fellow
Occasional grouch.

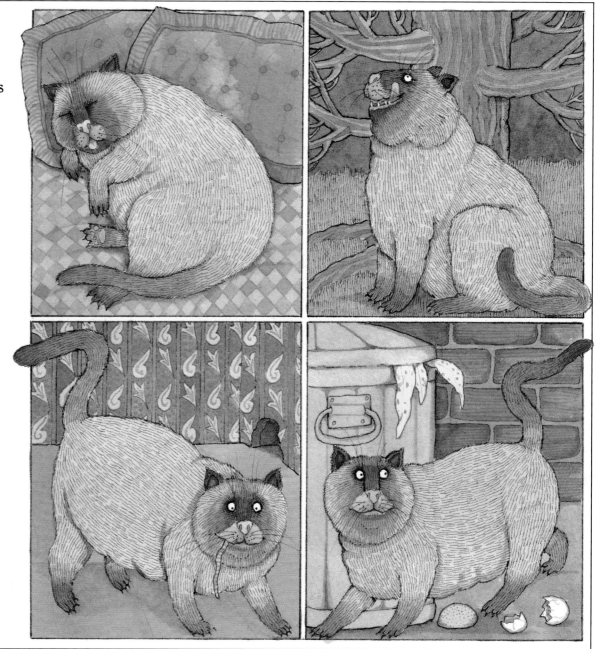

ALL EYES

Silly bird is Mr. Owl
Hoots a single silly vowel.

Lost in thought he sits there blinking
Never saying what he's thinking.

When he swivels left and right
Eyes surround the mouse-mad night.

THE BEAK
OF THE PELICAN

She looks for wiggly fishes,
At least so it appears,
To stuff inside the suitcase
That's swinging from her ears.

And though she's very graceful
When flying round and round,
How *does* she get that faceful
Of luggage off the ground?

SNAKE SONG

Toad gots measles
Frog gots mumps
Both gots such
Disgusting bumps.

They so ugly
It's a sin
They be jumpin'
Out that skin.

Pay no mind
These creepy items
Close my eyes I
Bite 'ems, bite 'ems.

YUMMYHUMMINGBIRD

I shake the sugar water
And the hummingbird is there,
Little yummyhummingbird
Hangs on air.

And oh she's so excited
On her helicopter wings,
Little yummyhummingbird
Zigs, zags, zings!

I hold a golden blossom
From a honeysuckle vine,
Little yummyhummingbird
Please be mine.

What is that bobbing
  up out of the water?
    Mr. Turtle's noble dome.

What is that poking
  along on the highway?
    Mrs. Turtle's mobile home.

Why do those bubbles
  pop up in the river?
    Mr. Turtle is whistling a tune.

Why are the shadows
  asleep in the meadows?
    Mrs. Turtle is mending the moon.

AT THE WATERHOLE

When Too Tall Jim bends down to drink,
A bunch of monkeys sits
And weeps for him
Because poor Jim
Giraffe must do the splits.

He flattens out his legs in front
And back until he's ready
To wet his lips,
And yet his hips
Are still a bit unsteady.

"Don't cry," says Jim. "It's easy!
I'll be giving lessons free
When all or some
Of you become
As tall as all of me."

BLUEST WHALE

Happy, she sings a day-long song.
Mad, she makes waves.
Lonely, she races ships.
In the cold and deep she rolls alone.
For peace she sweeps the watery world.
When no one is watching,
          she blues the ocean.

For fun she blows her top.

RULES FOR THE ELEPHANT PARADE

1. Follow the fellow-phant
   Tied to your nose
   Tug on his tail
   Wherever he goes.

2. Never spray water
   Out over a few
   Spectators who
   Begin spraying at you.

3. If you should feel
   A thumpity-thump
   That's just a fellow-phant
   Bumping your rump.

4. Once the crowd whistles
   And stands up and cheers
   Go right ahead and
   Start flapping your ears.

REMEMBERING
OSCAR EEL

He loved to scare
    A school of sharks
By giving off
    Electric sparks.

He'd catch a sea horse,
    Crab, or squid—
And oh the shocking
    Things he did!

At last he hid
    His grinning head:
His flashlight
    Battery went dead.

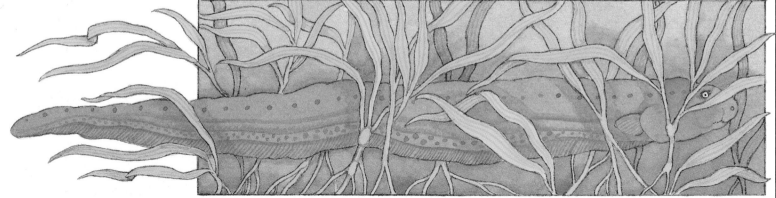

A Flamingo

is

a

long

coooooooooool

drink

of

something pink

BRAGGING
IN THE BARNYARD

The rooster is ridiculous
    To think that he's a prince,
The high and mighty boss of all
    The animals. But since
He wears a bright red pointy crown
    (Though it's a silly thing),
We often do mistake him for
    A chicken à la king.

TUT-U-TUT-TUT

It isn't some kind of machine gun,
It isn't a jackhammer drill.
The racket out here in the woods is
The redheaded woodpecker's bill.

It bangs on the bark of my birch tree
And rattles me out of my bed.
Oh what in the world's gotten into
That redheaded woodpecker,
      redwooded headpecker,
        rockheaded woodpoker's head?

HOW TO TELL A CAMEL

The **D**romedary has one hump,

The **B**actrian has two.

It's easy to forget this rule,
So here is what to do.
Roll the first initial over
On its flat behind:

The **ᗺ**actrian is different from

The **◖**romedary kind.

THE TURKEY'S WATTLE

Said the turtle to the turkey
Every time he came to visit,
"There's a funny hunk of wrinkle
Where your chin should be, what is it?"

Said the turkey to the turtle,
"Oh, this rubber decoration?
Heavens, no, I wouldn't tell you
'Cause it makes for conversation.

At Thanksgiving during dinner—
It's my relative they're carving!—
Silly people sit around and
Stuff them*selves* as if they're starving,

And you know the only question
They can think of while they visit?
'Say, that funny hunk of wrinkle
Round a turkey's chin, what is it?!' "

PENGUINS

Deep in dark
Antarctica
They waddle away
In their tuxedos,
Black ties and tails,
These little butlers
Who wait patiently
For a month
Of sun days,
Taking dips,
Dripping,
Flipping
Flippers,
Flopping—
Belly whoppers,
Keeping cool
At forty below,
Keeping everything
On ice.

THE NOISE IN THE MOUNTAINS

The yak is an old chatterbox of an ox—
    Not at all like the bashful bull—
And over the eyes of the sheep in their flocks,
    He's usually pulling the wool.

The way you can tell them apart is a snap
    For the fact of the matter is
The bull never bothers to open his yap
    And the yak never closes his.

Not a bull can be heard in the Himalayas—
    The bulls have gone home to relax.
The racket you hear in the mountains all day is
    The yackety-yackety yaks.

ROBIN

Suddenly Spring wings
into the backyard, ready
to play tug-of-worm.

TOM TIGERCAT

Tom Tigercat is noted
for his manners and his wit.
He wouldn't think of lion,
no, he doesn't cheetah bit.
Tom never has pretended
to be something that he's not.
I guess that's why we like him
and why he likes ocelot.

HOW THE RHINOCEROS GOT HIS NOSE

The very first Rhino (from Tokyo)
Just loved telling joke after jokeo,
   But he also told lies
   Of incredible size
Which is how he became a Rhinocchio.

OYSTER STEW

There's a squishy
Fishy critter
Swishing in my
Oyster stew.

Tell me, Oyster,
Mister? Sister?
Girl or Boyster?
Which are you?

THE WOLF

The wolf
  leaves footprints
    in the snow
      to show the Moon
        which way to go,
          but when the Moon
            decides to roam,
              the wolf looks up
                and howls her home.

A CHARM AGAINST
A GRACKLE

Dill, paprika, onion, clove,
   Rub an old potbellied stove.
Onion, clove, paprika, dill,
   Purple-necker, still, be still.

PELICANARIES

Pelicanaries are homely birds
who live among nomadic Kurds.
They cannot whistle, hum, or talk
much better than the clumsy auk.
They fill their bills with pitted dates
and Kurdled cheese from paper plates,
then sit beside the Kurds and weigh
the heated issues of the day.
And nodding off with croaking tweets,
They sleep on two too little feets.

RIVER-LOVERS

Beaver: river-weaver
Salmon: leaper-upper
Otter: water-swatter
Blue heron: hang glider
Turtle: whippersnapper
Bumblebee: humdinger
Spider: water-writer
Bullfrog: burper-burper
Owl: night-delighter

SLUG

She pokes along, this coatless snail,
Minding the unwinding trail
That glistens like a silver chain
And fades away in summer rain.

The window box wears her design,
Line by watercolor line.
Night and the artist almost done,
She streaks for home to beat the sun.

BLIZZARD BIRDS

The crested newt creep up the trees
With tubas swinging from their knees.
They softly toot a tune to keep
Their enemies, the snakes, asleep.
But what escapes these dizzy lizards
Is that the music, during blizzards,
Wakes up the snowy owls who hoot
And dance upon the heads of newt.

THE CULTURE
OF THE VULTURE

Great gobs of greedy beasts are flung
Across the plain, and there among
     The zebra herd
     A homely bird,
The Vulture, comes to dine.
    The reason why he sits and weeps
    and makes those funny chirps and cheeps
    Is not the company he keeps—
     The company's just fine.

No, no, the Vulture is upset
Because the Rules of Etiquette
     Were meant to be
     Specifically
For creatures wearing clothes.
    And so they know, when he arrives,
    Instead of using forks and knives,
    This skinny dinner guest survives
     By eating with his toes.

JACK A.

The donkey is an ani-mule
Who won't put up with ridi-cule.
His temper's short and, as a rule,
He's seldom very tame,

Especially if he's called Old Zack
Or Shorty Horse or Prickleback.
And if, of course, you call him Jack,
Don't mention his last name.

DRAGONFLYER

Dragonflyer, Dragonflyer
Stops in midair to admire
Twenty water spiders skimming,
Fifteen fat frogs going grumble,
Seven sunny sunfish swimming,
Thirteen honeybees and bumble.

Dragonflyer, Dragonflyer
Wings begin to teeter-totter—
Out of breath from counting water
Spider, sunfish, bee, and frog—
Lights upon her favorite log.

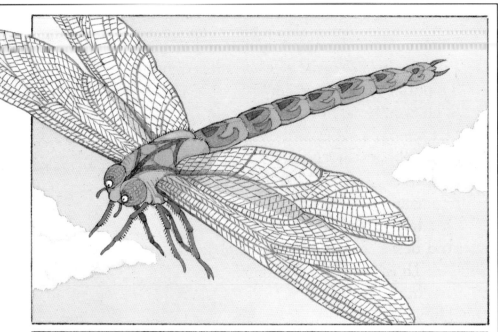

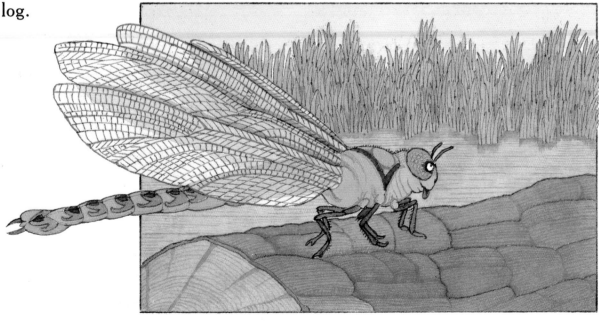

HOW TO TRICK A CHICKEN

It's perfectly obvious why
A chicken would much rather fly
    Or lay in a coop
    Than lie in the soup
Of a thick 'n' hot chicken potpie.

So a farmer approaching the nest
Had best make a formal request.
    To the hen he should say,
    In a delicate way,
"Do you mind if I help you get dressed?"

THE PEACOCK AND
THE PEAHEN

That hotshot strut of the peacock
Is a beautiful sight to see.
He likes to brag and wave his flag
    And glitter and chatter
    And flutter to flatter
That heavenly hen, Miss Pea.

Miss Pea is fond of attention
But very particular too.
She notes his pose, inspects his clothes,
    Decides if the dance he
    Is doing is fancy
Enough, then she shouts, "YooHOO!"

SIX BIRDS

The buzzard and the owl
Are God Almighty's stare and scowl;

The goldfinch and the wren
Are God Almighty's nod and grin;

The heron and the stork
Are God Almighty's knife and fork.

MRS. PRAYING MANTIS

Mrs. Mantis catches bugs,
Squashes them with mighty hugs,
Squeezes spiders even tighter,
Mixes them all up inside her.

Sad to say she isn't through—
She swallows Mr. Mantis too!
After that she sits and stares,
Folds her hands and says her prayers.

A HIPPOPOTAMUSN'T

A hippopotamusn't sit
   On lawn chairs, stools, and rockers.
A hippopotamusn't yawn
   Directly under tightrope walkers.
A hippopotamusn't roll
   In gutters used by bowlers.
A hippopotamusn't fail
   To floss his hippopotamolars.

The awful things a hippopotamusn't do
Are just
As important as the lawful things
A hippopotamust.